LOVE'S AWAKENING

by
Dhara Star Zyir

with
Marilyn Painter

Books and Products to help establish
The Global Spiritual Awakening

*This work is dedicated
to Neal, whose love and
devotion made it possible.*

Acknowledgements

I want to acknowledge and thank all of the Higher Beings that helped with this work. I especially want to thank my Master Teacher, Jesus the Christ, whose love is the Light that inspires and guides me. And E.K., my human Sat Guru, who woke me up. I love you all. Of myself I do nothing.

TABLE OF CONTENTS

INTRODUCTION

When I was eight years old, I felt compelled to write a book about the experience of existing in a world that wasn't right. The book was to be about very complex and sophisticated social and moral issues, such as feminism, war, and poverty. I didn't have the awareness at the time to realize that most eight-year-olds are not concerned with the unsoundness of the cultural infrastructure.

Throughout my twenties I experienced much inner guidance and made several attempts to write this book. I felt very frustrated, because I knew what I had come here to communicate and that this book was a part of my purpose. I also knew on some level that the time was not right.

Many powerful experiences have filled the last several years of my path. As I emerged from the dark night of the soul I knew that the time had come to write the book.

—Dhara Star Zyir

I had been asking for guidance in my life and it was clear to me that I was to begin writing again. We began one Sunday afternoon to discuss an outline, and the material which appears in Chapters One, Two, and Four was essentially that day's work, along with the message to us that appears in Chapter One, the message I cannot ignore. When we ask for guidance it will surely come; ours is the choice to follow it or not. My choice is made.

I am overwhelmed and honored that Spirit has chosen me to do this work and determined to fulfill this request. Each time I sit down to write I must give over to Spirit both my ego about my writing and my fear of failing at this task. I ask Spirit to breathe into me and use me as an instrument.

—Marilyn Painter

Those who have eyes to see and ears to hear . . .

CHAPTER I

The Journey Home

Amnesiacs we were, taken in and trained by our parents in the ways of their world, the world of America in the 1950s. We did not then remember another reality, but we were uneasy with what they taught us, and puzzled that they could not see themselves that something was wrong, that some vital piece of the puzzle was missing. And since they did not know, who was to guide us?

We searched alone for the connection home, fashioned talismans and invented our own ritual to fill the emptiness. Religion seemed only a shadow, unreal and lifeless. We knew reality was elsewhere and as children we spoke this truth in our innocence. And nothing could have terrified our parents more. So they redoubled their efforts to make us conform; this taught us the virtue of silence. They were afraid, so we were quiet. For the sake of survival we denied the expression of our Selves, repressed the female aspect, the intuition, the knowing. This repression bound/blocked/leeched our psychic energy and we tried instinctively to restore it. We took refuge in the earth's dearest manifestations, in trees, grass, wind and rain. We were seeking our womb, for we were in soul shock. We were evolved souls born into a plastic culture, a society of denial and oppression, so incomprehensibly different from what we knew. This very difference made us more vulnerable, for we were caught unprepared by a world so removed from reality, set adrift in a numbed, drugged world.

This was Dhara Star's beginning. And as we talked, it became clear that we had been writing, or trying to write, the same book. Marilyn dug up one of her beginnings, always attempts to describe that awful hole, that feeling of being alone in the fog. And this was the soul shock.

It is not easy to come aware in a technical world, lamenting the lost ones. Or am I the lost one, the one left behind? In the cold and mist of dreams to run calling, "Where are you? Where did you all go?" and finding no one. They called on me in my sleep once, gave me the key and called, but the key slipped from me as I woke and they remained hidden from me.

How did I fall from grace? Why do my hands no longer heal, nor calm the children? Why do I still ache in the gap that remained when my power left me, touching it gingerly, like a tongue probing a tooth socket? Knowing what I had by the hollow it left me, like raising a cup to one's lips and finding one's hand is gone. What separates me from my birthright? Where did I fail?

And then the message came: Awaken from your dreams, My Children. In time there is not much time left. You will be given guidance and support in this work, but you must hasten.

This is only a beginning. You are a sign, a lighthouse. This book is a signal to bring others here to you and to each other. This is a signal for a rumble of earth changes. A wave of transformation starts with this.

It is a secret, agreed-upon sign, made before you all incarnated. Those who see it will know in their hearts. You have felt a need to communicate before, but it wasn't time. Now the time has come. You have been entrusted with a key. It is a pre-arranged and agreed-upon signal by you two and the time is getting short. It doesn't have to be literarily perfect but must contain certain concepts.

You are a lighthouse, and now the light is being turned on.

CHAPTER II

Truth

Orphaned souls, stranded in an arid, barren society, we denied who and what we were. We denied our true consciousness, our awareness of the spiritual in all things, denied our inner reality, our blood ties to the earth and ocean, and our dependence on the Light. We started on the ego's path of self-hate and self-loathing. We adopted the artificial behavior and belief system of this alien society, as our parents had adopted us. We were not our parents' children, but orphans far from our true homes. The Western ego-world we found ourselves in did what it was supposed to do. It tried to sever the ties between us and our home.

If you are reading this, you are being called home. The time has come to claim your inheritance, your birthright. You have done good work, My Child, preparing the way. As you have increasingly cleared out the intellectual and emotional brainwashing that you have collected during your period of earth ego-incarnations, so have I filled you increasingly with Myself. Even now I am singing and dancing along your neurons. I am the spark of life with which your DNA manufactures molecules. Now you are being called forth to consciously and collectively work for the new world vision. It already exists and is being manifested into physicality. Now the world as you always knew it should be is here: a world of joyous friends and family, love ties, and creative expression in your daily work. The old world is in its death throes. The new world has been born. It is now inching out of infancy with the incredible self-awareness in evolutionary preparedness that a toddler feels when she begins to walk and talk. You are My Being. This is My Life.

The next step for some is to create centers of light and healing where masses of people can come to be deprogrammed.

CHAPTER III

Survival

For everyone in human form, until they wake up, reality is focused on survival and flight from pain and fear. People use all kinds of rationalizations and sophistries to hide the truth from themselves and others. They pretend to be sophisticated and civilized, but actually in their heart of hearts where their ego tapes are, everyone is a frightened little child focused on animal survival and feeling unloved, unwanted, and uncared for. These feelings, this experience, this false reality, are denied and then projected out onto other people in the world, on the concept of the "others." The victims of poverty, crime, the hungry, the homeless, those "others" live in an unloved world, but "I" don't. All of that is denial and projection because underneath everyone is terrified that she is unloved.

What's happening now is that the denial system is getting leaky. What does this mean? For example, people will vehemently deny that they don't love themselves, that they feel unloved, that they feel frightened, out of control, and at the whim of a chaotic universe. But just talk to them about their beliefs and feelings involving money. Very few people actually examine their views about it. The idea of money is surrounded by layers and layers of thought forms of scarcity and fear: there isn't enough; I have to have it for my old age; nobody will take care of me; I'll be helpless and defenseless and there won't be any money!

The flavor and content of this money tape is based on your family life, your childhood tapes, your cultural tapes. And the truth is that money is a manifestation of the Spirit of God just as everything is, and it can be used correctly or incorrectly. It can be used for the Will of God or it can be used out of self will. And eventually we won't need it. It's a tool.

So people deny that they are frightened little children, and act like civilized beings until the universe gives them a message and something happens to make them confront their denial system. And then their stuff hits the fan, because underneath that thin layer of denial about being secure, together, loved and functional, lies a terrified child in the darkness screaming for help, who has shut and locked the door on the one thing that can help her—God.

During the transition the increasing light and truth on the planet are going to rip the denial systems away from these people. They will be left facing their incredible feelings of emptiness, lack, fear, and terror. It will be quite intense. That is why it behooves you to start undoing the layers now, to go in and examine yourself. What is going on in your marriage? Did your mother really love you or was it her neurotic need to be taken care of? Did your parents really care about you? Did they encourage your individuality, your growth, your originality, or did they want you to become like them? The ego demands mimicry. True life, true expression and creativity, which is God, threatens the ego. The ego will do anything to stop it. The ego's idea is to cut off your arms and legs, cut out your tongue, blind you, stuff your ears, and then tell you to work from nine to five for the rest of your life in a job you don't like, save the money you're so afraid someone will take away, get old, be mistreated, and die. The whole thought that no one will take care of you and that you have to fight for your survival is ego. There is a loving God to take care of you. Babies know all this. All you have to do is allow Spirit to erase the tapes that have told you differently.

At the beginning, one of the ways you can tell an ego tape is if you overreact strongly to something someone else says. If you get angry because of something someone else says, you had better believe your ego is involved. It is threatened; a button has been pushed and an ego tape is about ready to run or is running. It is the same with feelings of fear or guilt, or any feeling except the higher celestial-vibrational feelings of love, joy, and peace. This may be a difficult concept for most people to understand; of course, it does not involve understanding. It is about knowing. Deep down inside of you, you are filled with a phenomenal amount of fear. The ego is the reaction to this fear and it has to go. You must rid yourself of the fear and you cannot do that until you face it.

So the first step in the process is to realize that there is more going on in you than you ever imagined, that the reason you are here has nothing to do with cars and houses, rent and mortgage payments, and making babies. If you are so together, why in your quiet moments when you dare to go in and look do you feel such emptiness, aloneness, fear, and lack of purpose? This is a spiritual emptiness, a spiritual angst. It is a hunger that can only be filled by wine from the living cup and bread from My Body.

So the actual first step is realizing that something is very wrong in your life, something very important and essential is missing, and then to notice how you react and overreact to seemingly innocent and coincidental statements and occurrences in your life. Of course, everything that happens in your life is a perfectly planned lesson by the universe to help you release yourself from your bondage and to return home. There are no accidents. There are no coincidences. Everything is perfect.

Now that you recognize that something essential is missing in your life, that you are having inexplicable reactions to occurrences and people, the next phase is to recognize and break through denial, which will be discussed in a later chapter.

CHAPTER IV

Birth

What is really happening on earth is the re-establishment of Christ Consciousness as planetary steward. You are living in the ego's world. You invented sickness, unhappiness, struggle, work, alienation, pain, suffering, hate, anger, and greed. These are the hallucinatory figments of a deranged mind.

The vibratory level of the human race increased in the 1960s. This manifested in the culture, especially in America, where the rays were concentrated. It has taken two decades to integrate this increase in light. Drugs were used to open the Western mind. The young people of the '60s delving into Eastern mysticism were part of the transition into what some term the New Age. It was nice to see My Children dancing in the Light.

However, at this point drugs are not a good idea for anyone on a consciousness path. They had one useful moment in recent time to open minds, but their continued use will alienate you from the world. They are a substitute for love; that is why they have become a mass addiction.

Since the 1960s people have been doing hundreds of clearing, releasing, and connecting processes. They have used meditation, prayer, chanting, rebirthing, Rolfing, massage, and so on. All of this has been to integrate the light from the '60s and release the blocks that keep us from knowing ourselves as Love's Awareness.

The most immediate concern is for My Children to reconnect to their inner knowing. This can be experienced through several sense organs and intellectual processes. Frequently individuals first recognize that knowing as an inner voice, instructing them in each step they need to take in their lives.

Don't feel disheartened if you don't hear a voice. This guidance can be experienced visually as well, and it moves toward an intuitive inner knowing, a feeling right vibrationally. My chosen teachers on the planet are surrendered to and guided by My Presence.

So if you are reading this book and are not yet consciously in tune with your inner knowing, the resources to help you do that will be pulled toward you by reading this book and surrendering to My Will. This book, like everything on the planet, is not what it seems. This book is a cosmic key, graced with the vibrational energy of Christ Consciousness, that will unlock hidden and repressed aspects of your being. Reading this book will be an experience of a great Aha! Things will begin to fall into place in your life.

Initially there will be a feeling of great liberation, hopefulness, expectancy, renewal, hope, anticipation, and aliveness. You will feel a sense of validation, such as "It's true. I *knew* something else was going on here."

Flow with this wave of feeling. Swim in it. Do not grasp or clutch at it, for this will shut it down as surely as resistance will. Honor it and let it flow. In fact, the whole trick to the transition is flowing. Both resistance and clutching place you in the hands of the ego. You are like a child's toy ship on a great ocean; you must merge and become one with the ocean.

After the initial realization, it is very important to be open to the external support that will flow toward you. You have no need to run off seeking external validation. Know that by the act of reading this and trusting your inner knowing, support will be pulled toward you. Know, too, that you have been in prison for what seems like a long time to you, My Child, although it is but short in My Memory. You are frail, oversensitive, starved, malnourished, unaccustomed to the Light. Be gentle with yourself, My Child. You have unlocked the cell door and stepped into the Light. Give yourself time to sit on a rock in the sun and enjoy the first taste of freedom. Do not push yourself too much. This is a time of transition, and as a starving man becomes sick from feasting on his first meal, your being needs time to adjust to the change. You have been starving for thousands of years and now a flood of nourishing love-vibrational energy is pulsing through your being. Also, be aware that for some, great fear may rear its ugly head on the horizon of your consciousness. Stay centered and know that the Light brings up anything unlike itself. This greater influx of light will act as a psychic enema and will purge you of unwanted debris and blocks.

Then there will be, and already have been for many, cycles of opening to more light, processing the darkness brought up, releasing and integrating, and taking on more light. Subsequent periods of processing and integrating may become frustrating. Know that you are erasing thousands of years of what I call de-evolution, but you term evolution.

Take heart during the periods when the ancestral and your own old intellectual and emotional patterns are being flushed out. It may seem as if a thick, black cloud has covered your horizon and the sun can no longer shine through. This is the time for faith. Know that you are just seeing the blackness as it passes on its way out forever.

It will be very helpful for you in this time of transition to align yourself with others of like consciousness in a support community. Alone or with others, those of the old world will just as surely condemn and judge you. Egos have much at stake in trying to retain the old paradigm in the light of the transition. They are digging deep in racial memory in an effort to resist the change. The change is inevitable. This is the epic when God walks the Earth in human form and meets Herself/Himself.

Remember that those resisting the Light are like frightened, hungry animals, but there is a divine spark in each of them. Honor their divinity, but do not take on their darkness and negativity.

There is a great gathering of forces; it has already started. Align yourself with the vibrations of light, which are evidenced by loving, caring, generosity, truth, honesty, forgiveness, tolerance, and absence of guilt.

There is going to be quite a bit of confusion in this time of change.

CHAPTER V

Inner Guidance

We have been talking about the need to listen to your Inner Guidance. The questions arise: How can you get in touch with your Inner Guidance, Spirit? How can you tell when it is Spirit guiding you in an interaction and when it is your ego? You will be given many, many lessons in this and they will involve very little risk. At first the choices will revolve around seemingly minor issues. Spirit has set up an obstacle course for you and you will not go on to the larger decisions until you have learned to listen to your guidance and made the correct choices on the smaller issues.

Learning to listen to your Inner Guidance is a process of trial and error. In any situation the process is this. Quiet yourself and surrender your little will. Listen. Act on what you think your guidance is. Appraise the results. You must be very honest with yourself in doing this and realize that at the beginning most of what you get will be ego answers. You are learning to sort out ego guidance and Spirit guidance. How do you feel? What is your response to the action you took? Do you feel gleeful or smug? If you do, you have been following the orders of your ego. Do you feel graced, uplifted, peaceful? You have listened to Spirit. You must scrutinize your own motives with impeccable honesty because once the ego catches on to the fact that you are listening to Inner Guidance it will try to use that situation for self-serving means.

Another feedback mechanism you can use is to determine where in your body the guidance seems to be coming from. If it seems to come from the gut (which most people call intuition) then it is probably your mind or ego functioning. If it seems to come from around your third eye then it is probably your Inner Guidance. In the middle of this learning process it may come from your heart chakra, but it is best if it comes from your third eye, discrimination.

If the "guidance" is the result of a cognitive process or the outcome of scenarios you play out in your mind, that is ego. If you feel the mental wheels engage, that is ego. The rational mind is ego. Your Inner Guidance is instantaneous, out of the blue. Surrender, quiet yourself, and you will be given the answer.

Your Inner Guidance may be in a form other than a voice or thought. It may be an impression or a feeling or a visual image. For one person, the things she was guided to do seemed to stand out in three dimensions against a flat background. Another saw lights and colors as a form of Inner Guidance. It may be as subtle as peaceful energy drawing you toward the proper choices. You may have clues that give away the source of what you think to be your guidance. For example, Dhara Star realized early on that her Inner Guidance never talked in negatives, so an instruction such as "Don't do this!" came from her ego.

These are only examples. Inner Guidance may manifest differently for each person. Try to feel the energy of the thought. If it is pushy, demanding, forceful, anxious or fearful, that is ego. If you are following Spirit you will feel very peaceful. The information will come in an unhurried, quiet manner. The experience will unfold with ease, no matter what it is, whether it is digging ditches, praying, or going to work. The results will be for the good of everyone involved, although you cannot always judge that because your ego gets involved.

You may be guided *not* to do something for someone and perhaps the person becomes angry. You may think that it could not have been your Inner Guidance, but that may have been exactly what you needed to do. Just be honest with yourself about whether you let interactions be guided by Spirit or whether your ego thinks that someone else needs a lesson.

Do not be attached to the results of following your guidance; especially at the beginning the rewards may not be that obvious except that you'll feel good. And do not expect reactions from other people to validate your experience. Dhara Star tells a story of when she was learning to follow her guidance.

"Spirit would have me do these things and I'd expect some kind of reaction from the other person like, 'Oh, you're a great saint,' and when I didn't get it I'd be shocked. Spirit would use different things for practice and for awhile I would be taken around the city. 'Get in your car, drive to this place, give these people a ride.' So I would stop and offer the people a ride and take them home. I would expect them to say, 'Oh, you're so great! How did you know I needed a ride?' They'd just get out of the car and say thanks and walk away."

Take a day and turn it over to Spirit and let yourself be guided. It is one thing to have faith and surrender and say "Thy Will be done" and another to then be quiet and listen to what "Thy Will" is. Surrender and then *listen* and miracles will start to unfold in your life.

Remember that God likes to work through form, meaning beings, books, experiences, etc. Your guidance need not be a lightning bolt. It may be a sudden thought to call your sister, or to visit a friend. You need the faith and trust to carry it out. It can get tricky when you really want to do something, say something to someone, romance someone. Your ego gets involved and starts to rationalize your desires and you may only listen to what you want to hear. If you are in a state of emotional unrest it can be very difficult to listen to your guidance. It generally works best when you are centered and at peace, although in an emergency situation a burst of knowledge often comes through.

All you can do is jump in and do it and know that you will never be put in a situation where you don't have the structure or surrender necessary for the situation where someone could be harmed. That will never happen. You will keep your training wheels as long as you need them. There is a built-in safety factor. As you get clearer and follow your Inner Guidance more steadily the issues get larger. The stakes get higher when there is a greater probability that you will listen to Spirit and not close down when things get intense or your fear comes up. You have to stay open.

Know that you have been getting information from your Inner Guidance, your Higher Self, Spirit, God, all your life. It's just that you haven't learned to discriminate between when you're hearing that and when you're hearing ego. All your life you've been getting guidance. It may have been to go to a certain school because you met someone who was very important in your development, or to take a certain class, or to go to a certain job, or to call a certain person at a certain time. All of that is Inner Guidance and it's been working all your life. Even when you were a child your Inner Guidance was working often, more often than as an adult since you learned to filter it out. So it is not something you're just developing now. Now you are learning to recognize when you are hearing your Inner Guidance and when you are hearing your ego, and to turn to your Inner Guidance more often and give it space.

What you are going to be doing is living your existence listening to Inner Guidance because that is what you are! You are not the form, the body. You are the energy, the Spirit that is directing it. Right now there is an imposter running your life—ego. Everyone is listening to something. It is either ego or Spirit and they both come as a thought or voice or images or energy. Everyone is always taking directions. The brain is not creative of itself; it's a computer and it is getting input from somewhere. The ego is a collection of tapes gotten from parents and society that say, "If X happens, then do Y." In a given situation, you can quiet and listen to your Inner Guidance, which might tell you something unexpected, or you can listen to the tapes running from the computer. Do you want a computer to run your life with input from your parents and your culture? Or do you want to listen to the Spirit of God, which is what you really are? Your form (body) is an organic robot run by a computer. You are not that; you are the Spirit that gives it life. You are the electricity that powers the computer.

Everyone is totally guided. All you have to do is surrender, listen, obey and have courage. Your life will be healed and will unfold. Basically, it has been the ego operating from the little will saying, "I'm going to do it my way," and then messing up everything on the planet for hundreds of thousands of years. It is really supposed to be a beautiful symphony, a dance with everyone interacting in certain ways and getting just what she needs and wants and everything being beautiful and peaceful and wonderful. And that is how it's going to be . . . again.

CHAPTER VI

The Open Door

Be still and know that I am present in you, My Child. The door is now open. Tonight we are going to talk about the ego. You must realize that your idea of yourself and the ego are one and the same. The ego believes it is you! And the personality you identify with is ego. So as you, using "you" collectively, start to consciously work at removing and releasing the old racial patterns of thought and instinctual, emotional responses, the ego is terrified that it is about to become extinct. Which it is.

So, My Children, as the door stands open and the light pours into the room, know that you will probably experience fear, perhaps terror. This is the ego's response to disillusionment. You are *not* the ego. The fear is actually a good indication that you are releasing old patterns. If you lovingly caress it and say goodbye to your fear, you will experience much less trauma. A very effective exercise to do at this point would be to write "My fear of such-and-such" on a piece of paper and then to dispose of the paper in an effective manner, such as burning it. This will bring immediate relief.

Know that your fear was a beneficial, instinctual, animal response for survival. It got out of hand; you lost your way in your fear. It is humorous that My Children are afraid of their own fear, which they created. But nevertheless, it is time to say goodbye to this old friend and foe, fear. It is being systematically removed from your consciousness, and any forms that exist primarily as channels of fear on the planet will self-destruct around the turn of the century.

The important and necessary work to be done on the planet is very simply this process of opening and receiving greater amounts of light, releasing old negative, constricting, and destructive patterns, integrating, and then opening to more light.

CHAPTER VII

Faith

The most important thing is not to struggle with your ego, although that is the most common response to it. It is nothing but a shadow, a black illusion of reality that has no substance. When one struggles with it, it is this act of fighting with one's own self-created fear that energizes the cyclic struggle. Know in your hearts that there is nothing to fear, that I, the Creator, am always with you. As a matter of fact, I am You, and You are Me. And the only veil between us is the shadow of fear that earth people often label ego. The most effective response to the fear that this book (and any other change agent you are using) brings up is faith. Know that you are merely cleaning the cobwebs out of closets long forgotten and avoided. Know that this, too, shall pass. You need to surrender to My Will, a power much greater than your own individual will.

My Children have been lost, and like any parent whose child is lost in the dark, I have sent forth multitudes of light-bearers to guide your way home.

The trick is to recognize the fear or fear-like emotion (anger, hatred, sadness, etc.) and to let go of it without becoming lost in it. Use prayer, meditation, and any other purifying device that you have used in the past or that you pull toward yourself during your time of preparation. If you choose to fight or resist the clearing-out process, things will only become temporarily more intense and more obvious. Continue to resist and you will eventually become exhausted and despondent. Eventually, you will realize you are powerless against your own creation (a fear, anger, etc.) and either surrender to the light or continue to spiral downward until you reach the bottom for you or you leave your body.

So, My Children, why not do something different for a change? Be easy on yourselves and surrender to the great influx of the Light as it floods the earth plane in order to manifest the new paradigm. Of course, as usual you have choice. However, let me reassure you that the world you so desperately fight to cling to, a world of poverty, hatred, and war, is going to disappear in a twinkling of My Eye. So, as the old earth saying goes, if you can't fight them, you might as well join them, because My Will is always done throughout the cosmos. And now, My little earth beings, who have hidden behind the veil of time in a nightmare of their own creation, calling for salvation, the dream is almost done.

Listen to your heart. Go to wooded areas, beaches, meadows, places where My Creation has not been as corrupted as in your cities: go to these places, quiet yourself, and you will feel the energy rising like sap in My trees in the spring. For spring has come for My earth children, a time of great joy and blessings. This is the birth of a new world, a birth that has been delayed, but could never be prevented. Know that all of this is coming to pass as has been prophesied. When your logical mind holds forth with excuses and criticisms in response to your faith, know that this is attempted brainwashing by an insane machine that has seemingly come to life and threatens its maker. You created the fear, lost your way, and became terrorized by it. And as I have always brought the spring without fail, no matter how isolating or frozen the winter, I come bringing the springtime of existence for My earth children. I am here now inside of you, growing stronger with each cycle of your sun.

Some may feel My Presence as an inner pressure to get on with things, however they may be at a loss as to what these "things" are. Know that it is your Self, your Being, that is being created, being birthed. Your conscious mind need do nothing but surrender and get out of the way. Birth is much easier and less dangerous if the canal is relaxed and accepting, and if there is a great sense of peace and faith that the process is in the hands of a higher power, that everything will be all right.

Dhara Star describes the cleansing process: "When I started consciously doing processing work to rid myself of my ego blocks, I had an experience one night of incredible love. I was up all night; I couldn't sleep. I couldn't remember ever having felt that way before. I was filled with love for everything, absolutely everything.

"I later found a book which talked about this feeling and labeled it a 'peak experience.' The book said that if you had a peak experience, you should just appreciate it and go on with things. You shouldn't try to pursue it. According to the book, there are people who have this spiritual experience of oneness with all things, and then spend the rest

of their lives searching for it and trying to recapture
that feeling. It becomes so all-consuming that the
rest of their lives becomes a shambles.

"I thought this was rather strange advice, as
though seeking that peak experience meant you
went chasing off into the fields with a butterfly net,
oblivious to and disconnected from the world around
you. The search wasn't some irrelevant adventure,
but the central force in my life. I became driven by
the need to process and clear out my life. It was my
whole existence. As I worked on myself I began to
have recurrent peak experiences. The more I cleared
out, the more frequent and longer lasting they became. I would go for a day, a week, once even a
whole quarter at school, living a peak experience. I
loved everyone and everything.

"It is an incredible state of oneness and joy; it is
feeling your natural state and it is all that you
want. This so-called 'peak experience' *is* really our
natural state. It *is* what we should be spending all
our time searching for and clearing out in order to
experience. And there's a pattern to it."

The first time you experience this sense of oneness, although your rational mind may try to ne-
gate it, you will know that it is unlike anything
you've ever felt in this lifetime. It is actually what
you felt like as a baby, though most people cannot
remember that. It is like a baby, laughing and coo-
ing in the sunshine, totally at peace, at one with
God and nature, knowing that it is totally provided
for, and open to giving and receiving love.

These periods of joy and love will become more
frequent and the intervals will become longer. The
catch is that every time you experience one your
being is actually flooded by light so that you'll have
a period of light, bliss, happiness and joy for what-

ever length of time is necessary to bring up your next step. It will last until it hits a block. So it will seem that you have periods of light and love, and then all of a sudden you'll be in darkness. Everything will seem horrible: your life won't run right; your relationships will go sour; and you'll be full of fear and anxiety. That's just the Light bringing up whatever needs to be purified. The periods of light and happiness will become longer and longer and the periods of darkness and fear shorter and shorter.

The experience is one of becoming increasingly in tune with your inner knowing. This intuitive communication becomes stronger, clearer, and less susceptible to ego interference. The heart chakra opens and this brings with it an experience of incredible ecstasy and love for everyone and everything. There is a pervading feeling of peace and a knowing that you are in the world, but not of it. Your relationships will be healed. People will notice a change in you and perhaps even begin to come to you for advice as they will sense My Presence in you. This is what religious mysticism refers to as "spirit descending into flesh."

This kind of processing goes on for a period of time specific to each person. After you have cleared yourself out to a certain point, you come to a door. This is the door of "Many are called, but few are chosen." You will spend years, or whatever length of time you need, in alternating periods of light and darkness while you work on processing your ego blocks, and then there will be a big change. The process takes on a deeper significance. This has historically been called the "dark night of the soul." This is where it is decided by the Higher Power of the universe if you are ready to go further along the spiritual path in this lifetime. It is the gateway to all higher knowledge. Relatively few have made it to this point up to this writing, but within the next fifty years, thousands of beings will cross this portal.

At some point during this initiation period, you will be provided with a choice. It will be between God's Will and your ego's little will. This will be individual and dependent upon whatever facet of the ego you have used to resist My Presence. Dhara Star experienced two doors, both golden and glowing. One door said "To God," the other said "Psychic Power." She went through the door labelled "God," and that is why she is My Mouthpiece and spreading My Word throughout the land.

During this time of initiation, the form will experience incredible ecstasy and bliss, very unlike anything experienced in the physical realm. The being will be very cognizant of the fact that something phenomenal is occurring, something the world never prepared her for. The person will feel at one, yet different from everyone, but there will be no sense of aloneness or alienation. If you choose the door that leads toward increasing spiritual attainment it will shut loudly behind you and clamor with echoes that will be heard throughout eternity. You are no longer a mere physical human being that walks only in a three-dimensional world. You are now the bearer of the seed, God manifest on the earth in physical form. Fetal and gestating, yes, not ready to try to fly with new wings, wings of transcendence and higher knowledge. But you are forever removed from the bonds of karmic enslavement. You have passed through the eye of the needle.

The next step could jokingly be called "the descent into hell." It is a period of reckoning and it is very difficult for most earth beings. So much of My Presence, so much Spirit has infused your form in the many levels of your being of which you little ones are still unaware, that you face yourself in a way in which you've never faced yourself before. All of your remaining fears, including your biggest ego block to My Presence, loom before you on your conscious horizon. The feeling of spiritual immediacy, bliss, and ecstasy is temporarily replaced by whatever ego issues you need to release. This is a very difficult period because people of the world do not understand and perhaps would even subconsciously block your progress at this point. It is best to keep your confidences to yourself unless you have a spiritual teacher who is guiding you through this. It is a frustrating time because the little bird that realizes that it has wings and can fly, that it's a bird and not an earthbound animal, experiences immediately upon this realization what seems to be a fall from the nest. You are now walking in the Valley of the Shadow of Death.

Know that you are not insane. Know that the process is natural. Know that very few of My Children will need go through this process unguided and uncomforted by physical presence ever again. By the time the majority of forms reach this crossroads, there will be enough of My Teachers incarnate to assist. As this process continues, because there is more "juice" enlivening your consciousness, your thoughts begin to manifest in the physical plane much more quickly. Since what is being dredged up in your consciousness are your fears, there is a tendency to manifest your fears and then exist in a state of terror. The remedy for this is prayer, meditation, and fasting.

CHAPTER VIII

Divine Will vs. Individual Will

There are many who are utilizing higher spiritual tools without being surrendered to My Divine Will. This is just another example of the ego usurping the place of God. Often what happens is that someone will use metaphysical constructs to manifest something that is her next step anyway, whether it be something as concrete as a relationship or a job, or a change in her personality. However, to prevent any difficulties or problems and to ensure that you are on the right track, the highest option is to ask for God's Will to be done for you. Otherwise, as co-creators you can interfere with My Divine Plan for you.

Know that I will always provide your heart's desire, your highest option, if you will only open yourself to receiving My Love. Asking for My Will is the easiest way to stay on the right track. Once you start becoming absorbed by ego desires you can forget who you are and your reason for being here, which is what caused the problem in the first place.

To ask for My Will involves an element of ego surrender. It is not until you realize that your ego is pure insanity leading you on a dark road to hell on earth that you are willing to perhaps think that there is a better way, that you are part of a plan that was conceived and instituted before a single atom was created in the universe.

My Child, know that there is a Divine Plan unfolding and that you are part of it. You can surrender your little will and receive greater happiness and joy than you can ever imagine or you can continue to attempt to usurp your Creator's function until the day of reckoning, which is very soon in Earth years. There are those, My little misdirected ones, who are using what could be called conscious thought to fulfill all their ego desires and unhealthy lust for power. Know that most of these beings will return to the fold. However, such behavior will garner more drastic consequences in the coming decade. Stay centered and surrendered and everything will go fine for you. Do not look upon your neighbor with envy because he or she has perhaps what appears an easier time of it. Remember that each of you has your own individual plan for salvation mapped out for you and that you are all loved and guided equally well.

Marilyn: This chapter seemed a direct answer to questions that had been troubling me. I had always been interested in psychic phenomena, although I had never indulged in or pandered to this interest. My interest seemed unhealthy and dangerous to me personally in a way that I could not define. I used to refer to what I termed my "inner guardians" whenever confronted with something new to see if it felt right or whether I should avoid it. I know that I have been safely and lovingly guided to those who could further me on a spiritual path, but I have not had the capacity to separate truth from untruth in what I heard from other sources. The only distinction I could make, and it was enough for me, was to know what was helpful and safe and right for me.

Several weeks prior to working on this chapter, I had witnessed a channeling. The channeler sat with closed eyes, went into trance, went somewhere, and another being entered the body. The voice changed, the facial expressions changed; it was another being. I did not feel the presence of Grace or Truth or Divine Being that I am conscious of when Spirit speaks through Dhara Star.

The channeled entity made some general statements about love. I certainly did not disagree with them, but neither did they strike me as great revelations of truth. Some predictions were also made. I did not have a feeling that this was "evil" or "wrong," but more a sense that peoples' energy and attention were being focused in the wrong direction. People were attending various channeling sessions, seeking truth or an authority figure outside of themselves. It seemed to me to be hindering their process of clearing themselves and becoming attuned to their own inner voice. The predictions, whether they proved true or not, also seemed of doubtful value. What was the point? The channeler was a sincere person, but was this helpful work?

Dhara Star's answer: There is a difference between expressing God or Spirit and what a lot of people are calling channeling. A good analogy for what I do is that God is the sun and we are rays. We are an aspect of God. What I am doing is connecting to the Source through grace and surrender to the

Will of God. What most people who call themselves channelers are doing is this: they allow an astral being to get into their form and talk and be. The problem with that is that you can only channel a being as highly evolved spiritually as you are. So if people have not done their years of clearing out work and spiritual processing they are not going to get a very high, remarkable being coming through them, no matter what the being says or who they say they are.

If you have Joe Blow off the street functioning as a channel, you will get Joe Blow's equivalent on the astral plane telling you their perspective of reality. As an example, Atlantis and Lemuria never existed on a physical plane. So if someone talks about them as having been a physical reality, then you can be sure that you are not getting high spiritual truth from that person. Atlantis and Lemuria are best thought of as allegories for aspects of consciousness. Predictions of Atlantis rising in the West refer to the re-emerging of a long-submerged aspect of our collective consciousness. Atlantis and Lemuria exist only in the astral plane, the plane of emotions such as anger and hatred and of millions of imaginary thought forms such as fairies and demons and all creatures the mind can devise.

Another problem with channeling is that the transmitting is done through at least one ego, usually two. The astral being has an ego probably as great as the person who is being the "receiver." Why not listen to God within, your own Higher Self? We were created to function in total surrender and obedience to a Higher Power, termed Higher Self or God. We are literal radio receivers for and the transmitters of the Voice of God.

To summarize, why bring another ego into the picture when you're having enough trouble with your own? Why not quiet down and listen to the still voice within rather than paying $35 for a psychic sideshow? Of course, if it's the psychic entertainment you're after that's different, but don't confuse it with God's Will. There is much ego involved in psychic phenomena. It can function as a substitute for real spiritual progress. Well-intentioned individuals are involved in a lot of psychic hocus-pocus under the guise of New Age spirituality. It is *not* bad or evil, just more ego. As you can see, ego revealed is insidious and boring. Channeling often is about money, sex, jobs, past lives, and having fun, while real spiritual work is often full of ego humiliation and disillusionment.

Question: Can there be a spiritual lesson in channeling?

Answer: Yes, it's a lesson just like any other lesson in your life. It's a choice: do you choose ego's little will or God's Will for you? It's not a better or higher lesson; it's just a lesson like any other and you can spend your whole life learning it.

CHAPTER IX

Karma

There has been much talk and speculation throughout the conscious history, or perhaps I should say written history, of My little earth beings about a phenomenon you label karma. It works thus: Spirit as consciousness decides to participate in the unfolding of the miracle on the planet by working through so much karma. The karma is the manifestation of ego patterns which have become concrete thoughts upon the planet. It is difficult to put into a physically bound conceptualization and language a more precise explanation. Suffice it to say that Spirit became identified with animal instincts and a very low level of awareness. This resulted in patterns of thoughts which all incarnate human beings experience. These thought patterns have energy to them, an aspect of life force almost. They are the closest thing to what Christians would call a devil that would seemingly exist outside of an individual's body. However, you must realize that you are not individuals. You are One Being, One

Consciousness, One Mind. There is nothing outside of you. So in actuality there is no evil, or ego, or devil.

My Child has lost itself in a figment of its own imagination. It's as though you imagined a play and upon acting it out forgot that you were the playwright and overidentified with the characters. This move caused changes in the set upon the stage that have to be undone, not because they in actuality caused permanent changes, but because that is how you find your way back home. That is how you remember you are the playwright. You retrace your steps by erasing karmic patterns. So when Eastern mysticism presents the theological construct that when you are no longer experiencing karma you are enlightened, or of God-mind, that is because you have undone enough of the karmic patterning to remember who you are.

To give a very concrete example for concrete minds, let's suppose you are born into a family of child abuse. Child abuse inevitably causes bitterness, anger, perhaps hatred, fear, and resentment. Those emotional patterns and their corresponding thought forms *are* the karma that you take on during that lifetime to remove from the planet. You take on the experience of being angry, hurt, frightened, and as you see through that insanity and remove it from your psychic being you expunge an aspect of that karmic pattern from your genetic family and from the earth. Certain beings take on large amounts of karma, as cleaning up and lightening the planet imbues grace. So what has been happening within the concept of time (which doesn't exist) is that the planet has become lighter and lighter, more purified over the centuries. The planet *is* consciousness and it is being returned to its natural state.

Jesus of Nazareth, whom many identify as the Christ, was one being who removed a large amount of the karmic patterning of the planet, but who also accelerated the process by the infusion of a new type of consciousness into the mind of the planet. The centuries leading up to the time of the birth of Jesus were in preparation, a cleaning and aligning of the forces necessary to receive the seed that was the Christ Consciousness as manifested by Jesus of Nazareth. So, My Children, the process has been phenomenally speeded up since that time, compared to what had occurred earlier. Now you are operating at comparative light speed as you prepare yourself for your cosmic birth.

It is as though you are individual cells in a larger body and you will begin to collectively remember that you are a part of something larger— not only the brain, but the entire organism that the brain directs. The God-Mind is the brain; the universe is My Body. You cannot at this point imagine the revelation an individual cell will feel when it experiences being part of a larger whole which nourishes and communicates with it. It is as though you have been starving because you wouldn't acknowledge the food that surrounded you.

There was a conscious consensual turning-away from My Will for you. Therefore, there must be a conscious consensual surrender to it. This is not a decree from an angry parent, rather a necessity. You, My Children, shut the door on creation, not vice versa, and only you can open the door. You are a conscious, living, divine aspect of that which you call God. You were created to share in My Life and to manifest all that is good upon the planet. You cannot partake of the abundance I continually surround you with until you cast off the false usurper of ego self-will. I am waiting with open arms for each of you to come home. There *is* the possibility that it could happen in the twinkling of an eye, however, the impact on the physical body of extracting the remaining karmic racial memories would be fairly devastating. The increase in apparent speed the process is gathering now is causing enough stress within the various levels of your physical being.

CHAPTER X

Denial

The consciousness on the planet is in the process of awakening from a dream. Denial is the soporific, the sleeping pill. Since all consciousness is connected, as each person breaks through the denial it creates a vacuum so that denial is sucked out of the consciousness and dissipated. It is like a ripple effect. Denial cannot co-exist with the truth. That is part of the process that is happening and will intensify in the mid to late 1990s.

Truth is love. People talk about God being love and that the universe is run on love, but their idea of love is a needy, conditional, emotional arrangement. Real love, spiritual-truth-love, *is* what runs the universe. Most people don't even know what love is. *They* know, but their egos don't know. It is very clean and refreshing; it's like sunlight. It's very dispassionate. It's objective and fair and just. There is nothing wrong with compassion when it is appropriate. Most people equate love with needy mutual addiction, then they get partially cleared out, open their heart chakras, and they think love is compassion and understanding. Love is much, much more than that. Love is a two-edged sword. And love also encompasses discrimination, justice, equanimity, and balance.

Compassion alone is not going to do the trick. The human race has to be weeded. The dying, unnatural, what you might call evil or ego processes have to be nipped. The garden must be weeded. You have to be able to be dispassionate enough to get rid of what does not function, that which is not conducive to the progress of the whole. Yes, it may seem like individuals will be sacrificed, but actually they will also be given their highest good. So basically, the ego, which you can think of as a darkness, will dissipate when the light, the truth shines in the room, in the land. Seeing through the denial is like turning on the light in your mental and emotional rooms.

The emotions you have blocked or stored around the denial are not the process you want to focus on. They are just part of the release. The process you want to focus on is seeing through denial. And the only way you can see through denial is to have the truth made known to you. So what is happening right now all over the planet is that consciousness, the Light, God, is making manifest situations so that each person can encounter circumstances that reveal her denial system. There are personal, racial, and planetary denial systems. For example, the fact that you feel you have to work for a living is a denial system. It's a denial of the fact that everything is provided for you, that the power of God flows through you and is at your disposal.

You must work on this process of recognizing the lie, the falsehood, the denial. Denial hides the real reality. Don't misunderstand or underestimate its power. It has kept human consciousness, divine consciousness that manifests as human, in shackles for hundreds of thousands of years. The amazing thing about denial is that you don't know that there's anything there. YOU DON'T KNOW THAT THERE'S ANYTHING THERE! It is the most powerful weapon in the ego's arsenal. You accepted a lie about who and what you are and then you forgot that there was even a lie. So the healing is to shine the truth. And the truth comes through beings who have seen through the denial.

So what is happening now is that the light is shining. Truth is being seen throughout the land and being manifested and the ego is getting very nervous. The ego system realizes that we are playing for its blood. Know that the ego would rather have you die than to have you live free again as children of God. The ego created death. There is no death. There is only change and transition. There is no death in the universe. So the process, My Children, is to work on your personal denial systems, of your family laws, thought forms, and fear. The lies are usually fears that happened because of a fall from grace. Then you believed in fear, which was a lie against the truth which is God's love, and then you forgot that there was this original fear that caused you not to remember who and what you are.

There are many who use various spiritual systems to reinforce their own personal denial system. Words can always be manipulated by the ego. Now, as Dhara Star and Marilyn have experienced recently, this book is actually a cover for a set of vibrations that are specifically keyed to undo denial. So as you read it your ego system will be undone layer by layer. And even if you have worked at clearing yourself for many years you may find deep, life-long false belief systems being uprooted and dissipated. This book is the truth; it shines the truth. The words, and much more importantly, the vibrations of it shine the truth. It vibrates with the consciousness of truth. It vibrates Christ Awareness, Christ meaning awake, consciousness. At this time on the planet, especially for those born before the late 1960s, you can actively work to remove your denial system to a certain point, but after that you need to have what may seem like outside assistance, such as this book or a spiritual teacher, to wake up. This is because the layers of denial are composed of thought forms that have been around for thousands of years on the planet. The denial is actually integrated into the very molecules of your being almost as if your spirit were encased in concrete. So spiritual teachers, enlightened beings, masters actually work as a universal solvent, a cosmic DMSO that permeates every molecule and atom in your being and releases this long-held negative belief system based on fear that is known as ego.

So what's going to happen during the great awakening in the late 1990s that we have talked about is that the consciousness of the human race will return to a closer alignment with its original state, its pre-fall state of grace. The molecules and atoms within your being are going to experience the vacuum process we talked about, so that all of the denial will be removed. Well, what's under the denial? Under the denial is the fear that was the original causative factor. We manifested into physicality, forgot that we were one with the creative force in the universe, became afraid, made up some lies about how things worked, forgot what we were, became very attached to those lies, and then denied the whole process in the first place. The search for truth is a removal of denial. Now, if this original fear was enough to cause the fall of the human race, you may ask, what is going to happen when all this fear resurfaces? If you do it gently, over time, it's like adjusting to anything. Your body will adjust to it; your emotions will adjust to it. It will just be a matter of cleaning out a closet and turning on the light. If it happens all at once, which will happen to people who are fighting what has been happening on the planet with every ounce of resistance they have, these people will self-destruct. Of course, by that time there will be several centers to which people will go to be processed and get support. But many of those who have not heard My Call to My lost children to come home, ever louder since the 1960s, will experience an almost instant removal of denial from their systems. This includes realizing that there's no time, that there's no space, that everyone is part of one great mind which is creating and watching its own movies. It will be rather unsettling. So, My Children, I strongly suggest that you begin your process now. The time within time is becoming short. Instant resurrection or awareness is not My preferred process but to those who fight and resist it may happen.

As an example, Jesus of Nazareth did not ascend into heaven in the sense of heaven being a place and ascension being a process dependent on time, but rather he awakened from the dream. He left the dream. He knew it was a dream; he left the dream; he showed there was no death. And the ego-minds of the time that had this phenomenon occur right in front of them made up a fairy tale, a linear story in linear time with linear events to explain the phenomenon. You are a rather stubborn and curious species. One of your own kind manifests truth for you, *manifests truth,* and you make up a fairy tale to explain it away, something that will fit within your ego schemes, your denial systems. "He's a God; he's other than us, and he ascended to this place, this physical place." There is nowhere else. There is nowhere; there is no space; there is no time. The limited time-space frame of reality that you call life, "your lifetime," is a dream. It is just like the dreams you have when you go to sleep at night. Except in a sense, your lifetime dream is less real than your night dreaming. A dream dream has to be more real than a non-dream dream. All you have to do is know this deep within the core of your being and you'll wake up. You'll realize that you are part of one great mind that is the writer, the player, the actors—all of them. *All of them.*

Know that there is no time and no space, that there is no ultimate reality. Knowing that you are one is a stepping-stone to realizing that there's no time and no space and no difference in the movies, that it is a movie. In realizing you are one, you can make mental constructs about being one with the planet, which is space and time, one with other beings during this lifetime, which is space and time. We're talking about a much deeper knowing realization. It's just a remembering, but its difficulty lies in the denial. It's about experiencing "knowing," Gnosis, the undoing of denial about things you have intellectually known for years. You can intellectually validate a knowing and still be in total denial. When you get that Aha, that knowing, that seeing through the denial I talked about earlier, the denial is being removed on a cellular level from your body and from the planet, from others. Every bit of denial, darkness, unseeing, unknowing that you dissolve occurs in you, occurs in your family, occurs on the planet, occurs in the universe. Each person has her individualized plan to break through denial. Freud did the human race a big service when he outlined the ego defenses, the emotional devices the ego uses to protect itself from reality.

The reality is there is no reality. The dream that you earth children have created has been such a horrible nightmare and you have been screaming at Me, yourself, for thousands of years to help you out of it. You are stuck in time, and what's keeping you glued to time is denial. Denial, denial, denial! If you want to believe you die, if you deny that you're eternal, the creative force of the universe is going to back you up for awhile. On one level you exist within the mind of God; and as the mind of God you can create anything you want to, except that I am no longer going to allow My Children to torture themselves. So, basically we have been undoing in the space-time of 2000 years what it took you a good million years to do. When you know the truth, you will realize that all this is taking place in the flash of a second.

CHAPTER XI

Guilt

We must learn to see everybody as totally blame-less and innocent. The reason for this is that be-cause of the way the ego works we cannot see ourselves as innocent unless we see everyone that way. If you believe that someone else is guilty, if you think that belief is justified, you have given your ego permission to judge yourself without mercy. This is not a conscious process, but it is what lies at the root of the ego's power over you. If you find fault with anyone, you will find yourself guilty and the ego will function as judge, jury, and hangman. So you must beat the ego at its own game. The only way to get free is to see everybody as guiltless. This is the key to undoing the ego's power over you.

Behind your denial, your ego is constantly sit-ting in judgement on you and its verdict is often disease. Consciously and subconsciously you will continue to judge yourself until you have forgiven everyone. Until you have extended forgiveness to all, your own feelings of guilt will continue to be manifested in disease, compulsion, and other self-destructive patterns.

Remember, your ego knows everything you have ever done. It sits ready to condemn you, holding a list of all of your supposed sins. Often the things on this list are what anger you most when you see then in others. If you judge someone else as guilty your ego will find you ten times guiltier. And guilt demands punishment. You project this guilt out into the world and pick scapegoats who are playing out your scenario. What you can tolerate about others will show your own level of forgiveness.

You must first break through denial to get down to this process the ego uses, although you can work on disrupting the ego's process by starting to forgive. Make a forgiveness list with yourself at the top and work on forgiving all of these people. They are all doing the best they can. No matter whether someone is a murderer, child abuser, rapist, no one wants to be like that. Every crime and abuse comes from guilt projected outward as anger. Having critical, judgmental parents will add to the ego's arsenal because that increases one's basic sense of unworthiness. You think, "If only I were better, if only I were smarter, if only I worked harder, if only, if only, if only . . ." It reinforces the ego's weapon of self-criticism.

Don't mistake how strongly the ego will wrestle with you when you come to break the final chains of unforgiveness. It actually is a death match. The ego does want you to suffer and die, then project it out and blame it on the world. Eventually, after years of processing you will come down to an intense struggle which had traditionally often been known as the "temptation of the devil." This is the final act in the struggle with the ego. The best-known example of this struggle is the temptation of Jesus in the wilderness. Since people could not handle the idea of ego, they projected it out to something external to themselves and called it Satan.

When you come to the final unveiling of the ego's remote control mechanisms there is a huge struggle. The ego does not want you to see its processes for what they are. Many people will engage in spiritual or psychological processes for a long time and receive healing, then their resistance comes up and they drop it. They may pick up a new technique and pursue that for awhile. They tell themselves that they want to be reborn, to be alive and healthy, but just before they reveal to themselves what the ego is doing they stop the process.

Do not underestimate the ego's protection systems. Your denial systems are so intact, so fortified that you have needed a guru or teacher or something that appears to be outside yourself to lead the way through. Eventually the planet will be light enough that people will be able to see through the veil of denial themselves but this will not happen for another twenty or thirty years. That is why there is a great need for spiritual teachers in the coming transition.

The final undoing of ego has to come from something you would never expect. The ego is guarded and has its defenses planned, so your Higher Power will set up a totally new situation to break down the final defenses. It will be something you would never think would be powerful enough to undo the ego. That is why certain spiritual teachers may specialize in doing things that are unexpected and unpredictable; this is called crazy wisdom. The final means of undoing the ego must be something really unusual to enable you to see through the despair and guilt that is the ego's creation.

Remember that Spirit is infinitely creative and can outcreate anything the ego has devised in its own defense. The ego uses ploys such as guilt, anger, and denial, but if you turn it over to God you will attract the exact counterploy to heal yourself. Nothing is too big for Spirit to undo. No matter how lost, alone or despairing you feel, ask and Spirit will give you the answer. Ask and you shall receive.

Know that I am with you even to the end of the earth. I will never leave you alone and despairing. Open your hearts and I will set you free, My Children. Nothing is impossible to the "I Am" that has created you. Bring to Me your tears and your fears. Come to My Light, those of you weary and broken by the ego's yoke. No matter what you are suffering from at the moment you read this, I will make you whole again because your true reality is love and wholeness. It is only because you bought into the ego's plan for damnation that you have suffered so. What has the ego given you but pain, suffering, loneliness and grief? Do you feel secure now? Do you feel loved and cherished? Is your normal state bliss and joy? Contentment and peace? If you have any feelings of sadness, loneliness, anger, despair or depression, even if only you know about it, you are under the power of ego. I am here to set you free. Come home. Come home to peace and love and joy and serenity. Cast off your shackles of despair. Open your hearts. Sing songs of love and thanksgiving. Know that you are one with Me always. Just ask Me and you will receive what you need.

Many people often become suspicious of prayers because when they pray they have concrete ideas of what they think they want. I tell you now, I give you what you need for your salvation, not what your ego wants to use to increase your time imprisonment. Know that miracles are being worked in your life even as you read this. The veil is being lifted, the water safely crossed. The storm is over and you sit basking in the warm and gentle sunlight of My Love in a safe and peaceful harbor.

CHAPTER XII

Judgment and Discrimination

Judgment is a function of the ego. It involves comparing, expressing rightness or wrongness, one-up-manship. Discrimination is a tool and a manifestation of Spirit which involves timing. It has to do with knowing when to act, when to speak, what to say. It involves surrendering your will so that you let Spirit work through you in a situation. It is nothing you have to develop. It is something that will manifest if you surrender your will to God. At certain points on their spiritual path many people are confused about the concepts of judgment and discrimination. There is some resistance to the idea of giving up judgment. People may think, "How can I not judge? Every moment of every day there are choices, there are decisions. How can I make them if I don't express judgment?" At the opposite extreme are people who are trying to extinguish their ego. They wonder how they can have discrimination because they see it as an act of judgment rather than as an act of timing.

Discrimination also involves giving people what they need instead of what they want. Many people use the concept of Spiritual Warrior on the spiritual path. This whole idea encompasses discrimination. It is acting decisively with your total being in the moment in whatever circumstance. The action stems from surrender to your Higher Power. You are expressing a higher will. This is difficult sometimes, especially for women in whom compassion has been overdeveloped, or who express compassion disproportionately to discrimination. Compassion is analogous to watering plants; if you give a plant too much water the roots will rot. Discrimination is knowing when to water the plant, when to remove the diseased leaves, when to transplant, where to place it so it gets the best sunlight.

Discrimination is associated with the third eye, the chakra of Jesus, the two-edged sword. As you begin to experience it working in your life it may feel uncomfortable at first, especially if you are coming from a position of being overly compassionate toward everyone and everything.

Know that if it is true discrimination, it is coming from your Higher Power. If you feel that you are guided to do or say specific things and then you hear a lot of internal chatter about that, that is probably your ego in resistance to the manifestation of discrimination. This will occur after you have a fully developed sense of compassion because you move from the heart chakra up to the third eye. Also for those who have not yet fully embraced their compassionate self, matters of discrimination are probably ego issues of judgment. Discrimination brings balance to your life. It balances the yin and yang, giving and receiving. It is as though Spirit abhors anything out of balance. If you have been overly compassionate for a long time, discrimination may take precedence in your growth for a while until you feel truly comfortable with it.

It also has to do with the courage and perseverance to follow your Inner Guidance no matter what manifests outside of you. As you begin to manifest discrimination your external world may become seemingly chaotic. You may feel guilt, especially if you have been overly compassionate, because you are not placating or taking care of people in an effort to assuage your feelings of guilt. So know that you may experience guilt. Just keep doing it and stay surrendered. Know that I am with you.

The spiritual path is razor-thin and rocky. Discrimination is like a laser beam leading your way. Compassion can lead you off your path into swamps where you become bogged down in needy, unhealthy relationships. Of course, compassion is the door to the spiritual path, but everything has to be in balance. And just as compassion is necessary, discrimination is necessary. It is the next step. More spirit will flow through you as you formulate and integrate a sense of discrimination so that no one and no situation can knock you off balance. You must always be able to surrender to your inner knowing and the Higher Will so that there will not be a chance that spiritual power will be misused for your own or another's gratification. You will attract to you many lessons and situations that will call for exercises in discrimination to learn to listen to that still, quiet voice within no matter what is happening externally.

This discrimination is very difficult for people in the West, because there is so little discrimination here. People in the West tend to go overboard on almost everything. There's no sense of balance because these spiritual principles have not been developed in their lives. There is no balance between work (or effort to express creativity) and play. Discrimination has not been taught or valued in the West. Judgment—comparing, condemning, qualifying, quantifying—has been substituted for discrimination. These are the trademarks of the ego.

Being discriminating may feel selfish or unspiritual at first, but if you see its effects you realize how necessary it is. It actually is a major ingredient in the dough that becomes the bread of life. Discrimination is like the little bit of salt you throw into the bread mixture to control the growth of the yeast. It may seem bitter, but it is necessary. It is the pruning and the thinning of the plants so that they will grow healthy and each one will get the nourishment it needs.

Discrimination is the ability to act without hesitation. It is knowing when to talk and when to keep silent, when to teach and when to learn. There is a perfect time and sequence for everything. Quieting the mental dialogue and listening to your Inner Guidance every moment in every experience is purposeful and fully productive in the larger spiritual sense of the word. Every interaction you have with another person exists for a spiritual reason and purpose, no matter what the external configuration of the experience is. Whether it looks like a business experience or a lovers' interaction it is all a spiritual give and take, a game, and as for superb athletes, timing and courage and follow-through are important characteristics.

This can often be a stopping point for many people in their spiritual growth because the accepted thought is that being spiritual is being totally compassionate without regard to the effect, results, timing. It is true that you cannot have discrimination without compassion because you have to open your heart chakra first and that is compassion. You must listen to Inner Guidance and the way to that is through the heart, but it is actually not true that what is good for the goose is good for the gander. Many people cannot resolve the idea of being spiritual and dis-passionate, but that is the only way for God's children to grow. You need equal amounts of compassion, dispassion, and discrimination. And they are all ingredients of love.

CHAPTER XIII

Security

Anything you do to feel secure is ego. This could mean your savings account, your college education, your relationships, your marriage, or your intellectual beliefs, whether religious or anti-religious. Whatever you use to give yourself a sense of safety or control in the universe is ego, for we are dancing on the edge of chaos. Existence is a spiral coming out of chaos into form. That's all there is and it freaks the ego out. Actually, that's why we developed the ego. The little computer realized it wasn't running things so it developed external control systems to feel safe. Institutions such as schools, medicine, and religion are used by the ego to define its version of reality—to try to freeze God into a static, never-changing form. The truth is that reality is always changing and if you hold on to one thing you're not staying with the flow of God. Spirit is always creating. If you bite something off and institutionalize it you lose the juice. Spirit is gone and you're hanging on to form. So all spiritual-intellectual belief systems are ego, and this includes all religions, pagan or modern, and New Age thought as well. You must undo anything you use to make yourself feel safe. It is all ego.

You all have on layers of ego, but the layers are different for each person. The things that are security to one person are not security to another. Spirit is walking everyone down the spiritual consciousness path in order to undo these layers. If you use intellectualism to feel safe, you may attract a spiritual system that intellectualizes so much that you become confused and your mind momentarily shuts down. If you use money to feel safe, Spirit will set up situations so that will be taken from you. If you fight the process, things will only get rougher, because Spirit will hit you harder with the same lesson. You were created to live totally in the present with no worries, knowing that God will provide for you. God does provide for you, and Spirit will use whatever is necessary to get you to let go of whatever things you think are providing for you and giving you security—man, woman, parent, bank account, teacher, whatever it may be. The best thing to do is to stay loose, because this process of detachment is what is happening and it is going to get more intense.

You also need to look closely at another aspect of security—being attached to patterns, to neurotic, unhealthy, dualistic, linear ways of being. Let us look at an example. If a person had a critical mother, she will have learned by interacting with her mother to have low self-esteem and to be critical. The person will not admit it, or perhaps doesn't know, but the critical tape and the low self-esteem tape make her feel safe. Spirit is trying to get her to let go of those tapes and will set up situations to push the button that starts those tapes running. If the person recognizes what is going on, she may think, "The universe is a mirror for what is happening in me. So if I feel so-and-so is critical of me and I'm angry with them, then I'm really projecting my feelings of guilt and low self-esteem onto them." Most people, however, feel better feeling angry than feeling their own low self-esteem or their own feelings of depression, lack of worth, and guilt. So they hold on to the anger. However, Spirit keeps pushing, setting up situations around them until they finally get that lesson and can go on to the next.

Another example is that a person might use physical illness to feel safe, because as a child being sick got her out of a dysfunctional family. As an adult she gets sick and suffers and that feels safe because it feels normal; it recreates her childhood. Good feelings do not necessarily make you feel safe. They only make you feel safe if your childhood was full of good feelings. If your childhood was full of suffering, low self-esteem, and criticism, then those are the things your ego will create in your life to make you feel safe. You have to realize that you have an investment in these ego tapes just as you may have an investment in a bank account. If you can look at the things that don't work in your life and realize how they make you feel safe, then you can start to let go of them. You generally cannot do this alone, but you can ask Spirit to help you get rid of the patterns. Therapy may help you intellectually realize what your patterns are, but you will never get rid of them yourself. The patterns are too ingrained; they are in your molecules. You have a terrified child inside of you who uses low self-esteem and criticism or some other unhealthy pattern to feel safe and nothing you do can make that child give up what she sees as her safety.

You have to surrender your will and the pattern to Spirit. You can work on any destructive attribute—bigotry, stinginess, being judgmental. Anything that you see a lot of in the world or that makes you angry is probably reflecting a pattern in you that you need to release. If you think that a lot of people are critical of you that is only your own low self-esteem projected outward. That is how your ego uses these patterns to allow you to feel safe. You might be so removed from the ego process that you don't see it, and intellectually you would find the process sick. No one in her right mind would use suffering to feel safe, but that is what you do if your childhood was full of suffering.

We have been talking about releasing patterns most people would recognize as unhealthy, but be aware that one of the biggest ego protections that hinders people from living totally in Spirit is the so-called spiritual path itself. Anything you do repetitively blocks Spirit, and spiritual ego is the last thing most people work on. They walk on what they call the spiritual/consciousness path. Spirit says to give up money. "No problem," they say, "I'm on the spiritual path. God will take care of me." And money goes. Spirit says to give up all needy, unhealthy, co-dependent relationships. "No problem," they say, "I have a relationship with God." The relationships go. Give up intellectual ego. Give up college. "No problem, I'm going for enlightenment." Then a real teacher comes. Give up your ideas about enlightenment. "OK, I know that it's only words. I'll be like you." Give up your idea about being like me. Give up your ideas of God. Give up your ideas of what spiritual is. Everything has to go.

This last bit is where many people get stuck. People who would never buy into intellectual ego get lost in spiritual ego. Many people are talking about getting rid of the ego and are living spiritual ego. Why? Because they are using their spiritual path to feel safe in the universe! They have formed a closed little universe and are using New Age thought, Christianity, Buddhism, Hinduism and other religions to keep themselves locked inside there. It is all ego. What we are doing has nothing to do with religion and is quickly having little to do with a lot of spiritual paths. The spiritual paths get institutionalized very fast and you are told to eat a special diet, be celibate, meditate, or practice other special disciplines. These are techniques that can help you get rid of ego layers, but if you begin using the technique or belief itself to make you feel safe it turns into ego.

Never get dependent on anything outside your Higher Self, Spirit. Any belief system has to go. You can take any technique and make it ego. Techniques are to strip you down so you can become like little children and dance with life. Little children don't spend time worrying. The process is to get you connected to your Inner Guidance so that you depend on that and feel safe enough to drop all ego protections. So as children we need to have a sense of wonder and not to rely on anything other than our connection to the Source. You just have to feel safe because you are. When you are in the Light, connected to your inner knowing and walking in grace, you feel safe. You have to surrender to the Higher Will, not your own will, and when you do you feel safe.

Many people have been confused about what the ego is and consequently, about the nature of their spiritual path. Ego is not being "mean" or material-istic. Ego is anything you do to feel safe on the phys-ical plane other than your natural feeling of being safe which comes from your connection with the universe. For example, most men are too dispassion-ate, too removed; they need to learn compassion. For them, ego is remoteness because it makes them feel safe and being emotional makes them feel afraid. Their lesson and their spiritual path is the way of compassion. Most women are already compassion-ate; they love everybody, give their power away, are martyrs, are "nice" to everyone. That is ego because being compassionate makes them feel safe. So their lesson and spiritual path is to learn discrimination and many will think that feels like ego because it's "mean."

Maybe someone has lots of money and uses money to feel secure in the world. That is ego. Her spiritual path is to give up things. Well, that sounds like a traditional spiritual path. But maybe some-one else came from poverty and only feels good when she has no money. Not being able to open and receive money and things is ego for her. For her the spiritual path is abundance.

People want to think materialism is ego and non-materialism is spiritual but that is only true for some people. The opposite is true for others and there are a thousand variations in between. It is the same for compassion and discrimination. People want to think being spiritual is being compassion-ate and loving. It is not true, especially for women. This is not the spiritual path for most women. It has been said that more women are on the spiritual path and more men make it to enlightenment be-cause women are too attached to men. The truth is that the traditional spiritual path is built for men; it works on building compassion. That kind of path makes women sicker; it gives them more ego. Women don't need to learn to be subservient, giving to all, compassionate. They need to learn discrimination, to own their power, to be assertive, to weed the garden, to wield the two-edged sword. The consciousness path is individual and everyone gets her own lessons. They aren't the same for any two people. So it is not true to say that you will find God by fasting, poverty, and celibacy. You might need to learn intimacy. Maybe your childhood had no intimacy of any kind and you are terrified of it. For you celibacy is ego; your spiritual path is to learn to form an intimate relationship that will undo ego. Your spiritual path involves intimacy and sex.

Everybody has her own special path to undo the layers of ego. So for one person meditating may be the way and for another it is pure spiritual ego. A person may meditate three hours a day for 20 years and think she is very spiritual and what she really needs to do is go work in an onion patch or work with dying people.

You have to dance the tightrope and you have to be ready to do whatever Spirit asks. So don't take yourself too seriously and don't ever get concrete about your path. You have to undo the layers and to do that you need to turn the opposite way of the layers. So what one person might need would be very bad for another. Stay on your feet and don't take yourself so seriously; realize that it's a game. It is God playing with Godself. An important layer that needs to come off is all the ego surrounding devotion, holiness, spirituality. There is great sacredness to life, and this includes a sense of devotion and honoring toward your path. But don't set it in concrete. If you get too caught up in it it becomes spiritual ego.

You are supposed to be like babies in the sunlight, not worried about anything. The reason you have to let go of all of these things your ego uses to make you feel safe is that you are supposed to be in a natural state of safety and total dependence on God, the Source, your Higher Self, and not thinking that you have to go out and create something to take care of yourself. The ego is based on fear. Deep down the ego recognizes it can't control the universe. It doesn't create anything and it is terrified of this dance on the edge of chaos. So the ego creates layers of beliefs and patterns to feel safe, anything to help it deal with the fact that there are no constants. Everything is always changing and we live amidst chaos. We do not live in an ordered universe; we live in a chaotic universe. It is always creating form out of chaos. The ego world, the logical, rational, male energy world formed as a reaction to intuitive, female energy chaos. Dualistic energy represses the female. As you strip away these ego layers, eventually you will face your fear of the chaos, the void. When you get through the fears and actually face the void, you realize that there is nothing to fear and you can make friends with chaos and learn to dance with it. Shiva dances in the void with Shakti, life energy, bringing forth culture, thought, and form.

CHAPTER XIV

Surrender

You cannot resist what is happening on earth at this time. You can *try* to resist it. This resistance encompasses a fear and a constricting around channels of energy in yourself through which life force or grace flows. As more light, more grace, comes into the physical plane it will take more effort and be more of a drain to resist the flow. This constricting is like having clogged arteries on a energy level. So if someone is resisting the lightening process occurring now on the planet, she will constrict around the energy channels in herself, the energy channels which keep her alive and healthy. More and more psychic energy is poured into the block and eventually the form will get sick and die.

In each person's life there comes a point when there is a call to surrender to a Higher Power, to God. Generally, the call comes at the end of a very intense time of resisting and trying to prove that you can run your life from your little ego-will. Things just get worse and worse and you are still not ready to admit defeat. It is a very good idea to recognize, as early on in this process as you are able, that you are messing up your life, that you are unhappy, miserable and empty and that there is a lot of denial sitting on top of this. The longer and harder you resist the more difficult and dramatic your surrender process will seem.

People may say they are surrendered to God and to God's Will, and then complain that they don't feel anything happening. What is really occurring is that they are not really surrendering. It has been said, "Knock and the door is opened." If you really surrender, God, Spirit, your Higher Self will take over and start fixing up your life. Your life will steadily move on toward greater joy, happiness, ecstasy, health, and an abundance of all good things. Things may seem a little rocky right after your surrender, but that is because you have made such a mess of things up to this point. Especially as you get close to surrendering, your ego is very invested in trying to prove to you that it can run your life. But what it really does is ruin your life. So until you have really faced the fact that the ego is completely screwing up your life and that you really don't know what you're doing, you can't surrender. You have to really know deep in your heart and soul that you are incapable of running your life successfully from your little will. Once you realize that, which is the process called bottoming, you may actually experience a state of despair and depression, because as your ego senses your proximity to surrendering to the will of the Living God, it puts up a real struggle. Your ego redoubles its efforts at denial and at whatever your individual ego uses to instill fear in you. So, for instance, if your ego is using the physical plane to scare you, as you get closer to surrendering you may get sicker. Your ego is making you sick to cause fear so that you'll stop what you're doing, which is progressing on your spiritual path. Your ego does not want you to progress on your spiritual path because it means the death of the ego. If your ego uses financial situations to instill fear in you, as you get closer to surrendering your ego will probably sabotage your finances. Your ego will do *anything*, whatever it takes to bring up fear, because fear is what causes you to constrict around the channels that bring the life force, the flowing, living waters.

If these words speak to you, if you are reading this book at all, you are probably very close to beginning to surrender your will to the Will of God in your life. Know that the minute that you sincerely and from deep within your soul turn your life over to God, dramatic and miraculous changes will occur. A very simple and powerful way to surrender is to say repetitively as a mantra or affirmation: I SURRENDER MY LIFE AND WILL TO GOD. You will have immediate results.

If you're in a specific situation and need help with something, just ask. Surrender your will and ask for help. It will be given to you. "Seek and you will find; knock and the door will be opened." Help will probably come through form, meaning that someone may telephone you with support and love, you may receive a letter, a thought may come into your mind to contact a specific person or service to help you, or you may be prompted to buy a book such as this one. Help will be given to you. At the time the guidance may seem insignificant, but in retrospect you will see it was a turning point in your life and a signpost on your spiritual path. Prayer is very important in the process and know that all prayer is answered. It may not be what you expect or want but it will be what you need. You can also ask for help from specific beings, whoever your favorite holy person is at the time: Jesus, Buddha, Babaji, Rama Krishna, Mother Mary (Virgin), St. Francis. Their consciousnesses are alive, functioning, and assisting with the transition. It is an important spiritual lifeline to receive assistance from your older brothers and sisters (older meaning more evolved consciousness). They will always help you. They have to; that's how the universe works. They got where they are because of their love. They will help you; it is their job to assist everyone in the transmutation of their physical bodies so that the consciousness of the human race returns to its original state as the Christ.

To assist you in discriminating between helpful and perhaps not-so-helpful people and institutions, know that no matter how good a story a person tells spiritually, she is only speaking as much truth as she is surrendered. In other words, there are a lot of well-intentioned beings who seem to be talking a good spiritual line but they are actually not surrendered. They are really operating out of their egos.

Surrender must come at the very beginning and is the fundamental basis and foundation for all spiritual transformation. Give Me permission to bring the Light to the darkness and know that I will.

Be still and know that I am with you always. I created you. I am with you until the ends of the earth. My time is at hand. This is the passage into light, into truth. No darkness will lie hidden. Open your eyes and see; open your ears and hear. My song is being sung throughout the land. My Voice, strong and powerful, is permeating the thought-plane of the planet. It is time for you, My little willful children, to return to Me, to come into My arms, home safe and sound, to forget the nightmare of hell you have created on your little earth. I gave you lots of rope with which to hang yourself. I knew that the temptation of self-will would always be there until you had experienced and chronicled the horror of it. I realize that it is difficult for most of you to imagine a world, a universe, full of peace and happiness and joy. There will be struggle on a lower level; struggle is always a lower vibration. But My man-being, My human child is evolved to the point to let go of the need for struggle. Struggle will still occur on new planets, in new life-forms. The ego phase of animalistic instinct is just a transition: self-will versus My larger Will, a developmental phase of autonomy. It has been difficult and seems long in your eyes and that period is now ending. You are now entering a phase of self-realization as manifestations of God the Creator. Next will come constructive creating throughout the cosmos.

Know that all this is happening in the blink of an eye. The time is upon you. This is revelation. You are not just created in the image of God. You are extensions of My Being. And now, those of you who are walking up the front path, opening the door to My house, it is time to cast off your doom and your gloom and your cloaks of despair and come running and skipping, singing and laughing joyously, into My arms, into the Light, into the sunshine. There is no more fear, no more despair. These conditions cannot exist in My Presence. They are anathema to My Reality. You must drop your layers of despair to be in My Presence. And eventually you will confront Me face to face. At that time you, My little pilgrims, will have adjusted to the Light enough to thrive rather than to burn. Know that My Consciousness is behind everything that is taking place on the earth today and that it is perfect.

CHAPTER XV

Hope

Probably the most important ingredient in the coming transition, next to faith, is hope. Since centuries of previously denied fear, despair, anger and guilt will be coming to the surface and since it will be a difficult and yes, painful time, there will be a tendency to lose hope and collapse in despair. This is especially true during times when you are cleaning out the dark closets of your self and you get lost in your own movies. You may feel overwhelmed by feelings of fear, terror, depression, or alienation. As stated before the most important things to do at this time are to surrender, pray, and meditate. And one of the most important ingredients is hope.

I am telling you now that all that is happening and will happen on the planet in the next ten to twenty years is the raising and the lancing of a boil. There cannot be a healthy organism until the diseased part is removed and the infection resolves. The human race is undergoing cosmic surgery, the removal from its consciousness of all elements of disease. That means all negative thoughts and all emotions, for your natural state is the condition of love. And it means all physical disease, all physical states of unhealth. A great purging is occurring. It is just beginning and it will increase in volume and in tempo.

Know that this is true. Find Me in your hearts. Be still and know that I AM. Stay centered and tuned in to Me within you and all will go well for you personally during this time. Do not expose yourself to the rising panic that often monopolizes your media communications. Focus on the positive. Pray, read uplifting literature, watch uplifting movies which have a higher spiritual message, listen to positive radio programs and music, and only associate with positive, optimistic, and surrendered people. If you must associate or communicate with those still lost in the world, full of negative thinking and violent emotions, know that you are being used to reach them, but do not be a martyr about it. Know that there will be contamination with their negativity to some degree. Keep this in mind. It is like clean water being flushed through filthy, corroded piping that has been full of stagnant water for years. In the process the clean water picks up dirt. But eventually all will be flushed clean and new and bright.

CHAPTER XVI

The Kaleidoscope

God chooses the hierophants, not man. Human-appointed spiritual teachers often don't have the juice, the grace of God, and are often operating out of their own will and their own ego's conception of what spiritual is. Sometimes the more trappings and approval by society such people have, the less truth they have to offer. There have always been public teachers and more anonymous teachers, and sometimes public teachers are false gurus. A person can desire to be a spiritual teacher and personal desire blocks God's Will. Some people who think they are spiritual teachers are just businesspeople; they have little if any light. Many people in everyday jobs do have the Light. Grace is given by God.

What is happening now, and has indeed been happening for some time, is that the spiritual baton is being transferred from India to America. There is a group of very high human beings who travel about the United States incognito, without the glorious trappings of secular approval, spreading the Light and the Word of God. These beings who are preparing the cities and the people in them for the coming transition are using the cover of New Age anyperson. So know that there are many anonymous teachers of God who are teaching fairly high level truth and knowledge and also know that there are people who describe themselves as spiritual teachers who are operating almost totally out of ego. Furthermore, it is a stage in the development of true teachers to go through a phase of disidentification with their ego, when they realize that much of their teaching has been coming from their ego, interspersed with the truth.

Therefore, you never choose a teacher by how much approval or disapproval they have from society, by how much money they have, or how many books they have written. You have to evaluate a teacher by reliance upon your own inner knowing and intuition about the person. If you feel freaked out by someone she may actually be your perfect teacher because she may bring up your ego tapes. On the other hand you may not feel good about someone and that may be because she is dabbling in the psychic and operating out of ego. You have to clean yourself out enough to be able to use your inner knowing as the final truth meter, realizing that your ego will try to confuse the process. There is no one who can teach this to you with words. There are beings who can help you experience it and help you validate yourself, but it really comes down to you knowing the truth inside yourself.

Remember that God is infinitely creative and that Spirit resists becoming secularized. The institutionalization of Spirit puts layers of ego on it and Spirit starts to withdraw. You have to experience going beyond all form, to stop creating form and experience. Spirit is crazy wisdom that will do anything so the ego can't outguess it, anything to shut down the rational mind. You must stop analyzing, quit reacting, quit copying, stop your obsession with yourself and your "reality." One way to do this is to get the ego so confused, so overloaded with things that don't fit into its past experiences that it gives up. Spontaneity blows the ego away. Let go of your assumptions about what "spiritual" is. Even the word "spiritual" encases what God is in a hundred layers of ego. GOD IS. Spirit is a kaleidoscope which is faster than light and the instant you tie it to something ego enters in.

We are a kaleidoscope of consciousness. Every so often God twirls the kaleidoscope and the seal of power takes a different manifestation. Two examples of this are the American Indians and the Hindus, some of whom were/are enlightened beings. These beings then had to try to bring the truth to their cultures. Problems set in when trying to express the formless experience with words. Language is form and detracts from knowledge. Language is of the ego. So almost immediately upon communication of spiritual experience the meaning is changed. It is as if light leaks out of a sieve, the sieve being language. Employing form loses content. Eventually knowledge turns into religion and becomes empty ritual as the spiritual light is drained from it. Spiritual phenomena begin with enlightenment and gradually become encased in ego. People are still following the old paths and there is still a little juice to some of them, still pockets of power left over, but they are no longer direct manifestations of the Source. Some Spirit is left in religions but God is bringing forward a new paradigm. It is like a light on a stage and the light is moving from the Hindu mystics to the West. We are the new paradigm; we are setting the spiritual pattern for the next thousand years.

So my final advice is: open your heart, trust your inner knowing, surrender to God's Will, and take a risk in moving forward on your spiritual path.

PRAISE TO THE CREATOR
OM

Books and Products to help establish
The Global Spiritual Awakening

A great shift in consciousness is gaining momentum around the globe. This book is one of many intended to help in this tremendous effort, the awakening of Mankind. We at Uni★Sun have been privileged to publish a number of books that will contribute significantly to this most important process. Please write for our free catalog.

Uni★Sun
P. O. Box 25421
Kansas City, Missouri 64119
U.S.A.